MONARCHY

LEEANNE GELLETLY

MASON CREST
PHILADELPHIA

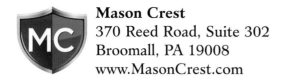

Mason Crest
370 Reed Road, Suite 302
Broomall, PA 19008
www.MasonCrest.com

Printed and bound in the United States of America

CPSIA Compliance Information: Batch #MEG2012-6. For further information, contact Mason Crest at 1-866-MCP-Book.

First printing
1 3 5 7 9 8 6 4 2

Library of Congress Cataloging-in-Publication Data

Gelletly, LeeAnne.
  Monarchy / LeeAnne Gelletly.
      p. cm. — (Major forms of world government)
  Includes bibliographical references and index.
  ISBN 978-1-4222-2141-9 (hc)
  ISBN 978-1-4222-9458-1 (ebook)
  1. Monarchy—Juvenile literature. I. Title.
  JC375.G45 2013
  321'. 6—dc23
                              2012027846

Publisher's note: All quotations in this book are taken from original sources, and contain the spelling and grammatical inconsistencies of the original texts.

TITLES IN THIS SERIES

COMMUNISM
DEMOCRACY
DICTATORSHIP
FASCISM

MILESTONES
IN THE EVOLUTION
OF GOVERNMENT

MONARCHY
OLIGARCHY
THEOCRACY

TABLE OF CONTENTS

INTRODUCTION by Dr. Timothy Colton, Harvard University

When human beings try to understand complex sets of things, they usually begin by sorting them into categories. They classify or group the phenomena that interest them into boxes that are basically very much alike. These boxes can then be compared and analyzed. The logic of classification applies to the study of inanimate objects (such as, for example, bodies of water or minerals), to living organisms (such as species of birds or bacteria), and also to man-made systems (such as religions or communications media).

This series of short books is about systems of government, which are specific and very important kinds of man-made systems. Systems of government are arrangements for human control and cooperation on particular territories. Governments dispense justice, make laws, raise taxes, fight wars, run school and health systems, and perform many other services that we often take for granted. Like, say, minerals, bacteria, and religions, systems of government come in a wide variety of forms or categories.

Just what are those categories? One of the earliest attempts to answer this question rigorously was made in the fourth century BCE by the brilliant Greek philosopher Aristotle. His study *Politics* has come down to us in incomplete form, as many of his writings were lost after he died. Nonetheless, it contains a simple and powerful scheme for classifying systems of government. Aristotle researched and illustrated his treatise by looking at the constitutions of 158 small city-states near the eastern shores of the Mediterranean Sea of his day, most of them inhabited by Greeks.

According to Aristotle's *Politics*, any system of government could be accurately classified and thus understood once two things were known. The first was, how many people were involved in making political decisions: one person, a small number, or a large number. The second issue was whether the system was designed to serve the common good of the citizens of the city-state. Taken together, these distinctions produced six categories of governmental system in all: monarchy (rule by one civic-minded person); tyranny (rule by one selfish person); aristocracy (rule by the few in the interests of all); oligarchy (rule by the few to suit themselves); constitutional government or "polity" (rule by the many in the common interest); and finally a form of mob rule (rule by the many with no concern for the greater good).

The fifth of these classic categories comes closest to modern representative democracy, as it is experienced in the United States, Western Europe, India, and many other places. One of the things Aristotle teaches us, however, is that there are many alternatives to this setup. In addition to the volume on democracy, this Mason Crest series will acquaint students with systems of government that correspond in rough terms to other categories invented by Aristotle more than two thousand years ago. These include monarchy; dictatorship (in Aristotle's terms, tyranny); oligarchy; communism (which we might think of as a particular kind of modern-day oligarchy); fascism (which combines some of the characteristics of tyranny and mob rule); and theocracy (which does not fit easily into Aristotle's scheme, although we might think of it as tyranny or oligarchy, but in the name of some divine being or creed).

Aristotle focused his research on the written constitutions of city-states. Today, political scientists, with better tools at their disposal, delve more into the actual practice of government in different countries. That practice frequently differs from the theory written into the constitution. Scholars study why it is that countries differ so much in terms of how and in whose interests governmental decisions are taken, across broad categories and within these categories, as well as in mixed systems that cross the boundaries between categories. It turns out that there are not one but many reasons for these differences, and there are significant disagreements about which reasons are most important. Some of the reasons are examined in this book series.

Experts on government also wonder a lot about trends over time. Why is it that some version of democracy has come to be the most common form of government in the contemporary world? Why has democratization come in distinct waves, with long periods of stagnation or even of reverse de-democratization separating them? The so-called third wave of democratization began in the 1970s and extended into the 1990s, and featured, among other changes, the collapse of communist systems in the Soviet Union and Eastern Europe and the disintegration of differently constituted nondemocratic systems in Southern Europe and Latin America. At the present time, the outlook for democracy is uncertain. In a number of Arab countries, authoritarian systems of government have recently been overthrown or challenged by revolts. And yet, it is far from clear that the result will be functioning democracies. Moreover, it is far from clear that the world will not encounter another wave of de-democratization. Nor can we rule out the rise of fundamentally new forms of government not foreseen by Aristotle; these might be encouraged by contemporary forms of technology and communication, such as the Internet, behavioral tracking devices, and social media.

For young readers to be equipped to consider complex questions like these, they need to begin with the basics about existing and historical systems of government. It is to meet their educational needs that this book series is aimed.

Prince William and his new bride, Kate Middleton, greet a crowd of well-wishers after their wedding, April 29, 2011.

1

TRADITIONS OF THE MONARCHY

In the spring of 2011 an estimated 2 billion people around the world were riveted by a televised wedding. The event, attended by 1,900 guests, took place with pomp and pageantry and images of scarlet-and-gold uniformed soldiers on horseback before an old Gothic church. It was a royal wedding, held at the 700-year-old Westminster Abbey, in London, England.

When the ceremony was over, 28-year-old Prince William, Duke of Cambridge, had wed Catherine "Kate" Middleton. With their marriage, Kate, who has no royal blood, became a duchess and a member of the royal family. The wedding thrilled the estimated one million people who thronged the streets outside the abbey, as well as millions more who celebrated at parties in England that night. The royal wedding allowed them to show support for the British monarchy, an English institution that dates back more than a thousand years.

William is a member of the Windsor dynasty. His grandparents are Queen Elizabeth II—who currently sits on the British throne—and Philip, the Duke of Edinburgh. His father, Charles, the Prince of Wales, is first in line for the throne upon the death of the queen. William is second in line to the British throne.

WHAT IS A MONARCHY?

The titles of king and queen, prince and princess, duke and duchess, earl and countess are used in a form of government known as a monarchy. The word *monarchy* comes from the Greek language: *monarkhia* means "rule of one." In a monarchy, a sovereign serves as head of state, holding power until his or her death or abdication.

The title of a male monarch may be king, emperor, shah, caliph, sultan, emir, or tsar, while the title of a female leader is usually queen or empress. Monarchs differ from other heads of state, such as presidents, because their position is typically unelected and held for life.

Rules of succession determine who is to be the next king or queen. In many cases, succession is determined by primogeniture. This is a system of hereditary monarchy in which the eldest child is first in line to the throne. In the past, patrilineal primogeniture was the rule in most countries with monarchies. This meant only sons could ascend to the throne.

The right to rule is sometimes based on proximity of blood, or closeness in degree of kinship. In such cases a younger brother or nephew succeeds the king. When a succession of rulers of a kingdom or

KEY IDEA

A monarchy is a form of government in which a sovereign ruler, usually determined by hereditary succession and usually serving for life, is head of state. The powers of most monarchies today are limited by constitutions or parliaments.

Queen Elizabeth II and her husband, Prince Philip, the Duke of Edinburgh, wave from the balcony at Buckingham Palace in London, June 2012. While the wife of a king is typically given the title of queen, the husband of a queen is referred to as the "prince consort," not as king.

nation are related to or are members of the same family, they are considered part of a dynasty.

Rules of succession were designed to ensure continuity of leadership and government stability. When a monarch died, everyone knew who would lead next. This prevented potentially violent struggles for power. In England, acceptance of the rules of succession was expressed by the statement "The King is dead. Long live the King!"

Monarchy evolved in human history as states became larger and more complex. It allowed for strong, centralized government. History offers many examples of kings and queens who ruled effectively, bringing benefits to their societies. But there are also many examples of weak, frivolous,

In February 2012 Queen Elizabeth II celebrated 60 years on the British throne. She ascended to the throne on February 6, 1952, upon the death of her father. Sixteen months later, in June 1953, the religious service of her coronation was held at Westminster Abbey.

or corrupt monarchs whose reigns proved disastrous. Such cases show the weakness of a system in which governing authority is treated as a birthright.

FORMS OF MONARCHIES

Monarchies are not all the same. The power of a sovereign can vary from nation to nation.

An absolute monarchy is a monarchy that is not limited by the laws or constitution of the nation. The head of state holds absolute authority. He or she has the power to make, enforce, and interpret the laws, as well as determine punishments. In an absolute monarchy the king or queen rules by decree and answers to no judicial, legislative, religious, or electoral body.

A constitutional monarchy is a system of government in which the monarch has limited powers, which are specified by the nation's constitution or laws. In such systems, the authority to create new laws rests with a parliament, assembly, or some other legislative body. Usually the head of government is a prime minister, chief minister, or premier. In some constitutional monarchies today, the monarch has significant powers (for example, the authority to dissolve the legislature or veto laws). But in most cases the king or queen is a figurehead who performs only ceremonial functions.

In addition to being a constitutional monarchy, the United Kingdom is also a parliamentary democracy. The British Parliament is a legislative body with two chambers: the House of Commons and the House of Lords. Most laws originate in the House of Commons, whose 650 members are elected by the people. The head of the political party with the majority of seats in the House of Commons is the prime minister. Parliament's other chamber, the House of Lords, revises and approves legislation. It has approximately 825 members (the exact number can vary at any given time). In the past, the House of Lords was the exclusive domain of the aristocracy: only those with an inherited title of nobility had seats. Today, most members of the House of Lords are appointed and have "life peerages"—titles, conferred by the monarch for exceptional achievement, that cannot be passed on to children.

THE ARISTOCRACY

Throughout history, monarchs governed countries with the help of family members and a small class of wealthy elites, known as the aristocracy. The aristocracy, which was usually made up of the hereditary nobility, might manage estates, control the military, or collect taxes. Other nobles served as advisers to the monarch or helped deal with affairs of the country, including its finances, foreign relations, defense, and laws.

This ruling class, along with the king's advisers and courtiers, made up the royal court. A monarch typically "held court" at the sovereign's official residence, the palace. But politics was not the only focus. Royal courts were also places where new ideas in literature, science, and fashion would be discussed and displayed. Royal families and the aristocracy also established rites and rituals that formed the traditions of a monarchy.

As the oldest child of Queen Beatrix of the Netherlands, Willem-Alexander is the heir apparent, or next in line, to the throne of that kingdom. His current title, crown prince, reflects his position in the hierarchy of succession in the Netherlands.

SYMBOLS, RITES, AND RITUALS

One of the most important traditions is the coronation ceremony, a ritual that officially authorizes a monarch's right to rule. Coronations often have a religious component. In Britain, for example, the Archbishop of Canterbury—the senior bishop and principal leader of the Church of England—presides over the ceremony.

The ritual typically includes the use of certain "crown jewels"—the crowns, ornaments, and other jewelry acquired during the existence of the institution. These items can be of great value, skillfully crafted of gold or silver and studded with precious gems. Crown jewels are also worn or carried for state occasions. Such regalia serve the purpose of connecting the present ruler with the history and traditions of the past. Their use represents the continuity of the monarchy.

Sultan Qaboos bin Said of Oman is an absolute monarch. He controls all powers of government, and his authority is not limited by a constitution or set of laws.

In Britain, the coronation ritual has remained basically the same for a thousand years. It begins with the new sovereign being presented to and acclaimed by the people. After being shown certain crown jewels symbolizing the authority of the monarchy, the new king or queen is asked to swear an oath promising to uphold the law, justice, and the Church. After affirming the oath, the monarch is anointed with oil, presented with more regalia, and crowned. Afterward, the new king or queen receives oaths of loyalty, or homage, from subjects of the realm.

At the coronation of Queen Elizabeth II, held in June 1953, the archbishop placed St. Edward's crown (created in 1661) on her head. At the end of the ceremony, she removed the coronation crown and replaced it with the Imperial State Crown. Wearing that crown, she walked out of Westminster Abbey carrying in her left hand a hollow golden sphere, called the Sovereign's Orb, and a jewel-ornamented golden rod, called the Scepter with the Cross, in her right.

The queen also wears the Imperial State Crown on occasions such as the State Opening of Parliament. This annual ritual, which follows a centuries-old tradition, requires the monarch to deliver before Parliament a speech on the country's plans and future laws. The speech is written by the prime minister.

The royal coat of arms of the United Kingdom includes symbols that represent the lands ruled by the monarch: the lion (England), unicorn (Scotland), and a harp (Northern Ireland).

Another symbol of the monarchy is the royal coat of arms—the shield representing the British monarchy. Because the duty of a ruler is to guarantee that justice is done, the royal coat of arms appears in courtrooms throughout the United Kingdom.

Details of the coat of arms also appear on coins that feature the portrait of the queen. An important symbol of the monarchy is the image of its sovereign. Early civilizations used statues and monuments to represent the

The temples, monuments, and palaces built or used by a ruler are another indication of a monarch's power and authority. In Britain, the official residences of the queen include Buckingham Palace, in London; Windsor Castle, in Berkshire, England; and the Palace of Holyroodhouse, in Edinburgh, Scotland.

power of the monarchy. Later kingdoms issued coins and paper money stamped with a sovereign's portrait as proof of his or her authority. Today, the image of Queen Elizabeth appears on coins, paper currency, and stamps.

In constitutional monarchies the sovereign and his or her family often play a ceremonial role in many of the country's military, political, and diplomatic functions. For many people they are a symbol of their nation's cultural identity.

2

ANCIENT MONARCHIES

Monarchy is one of the oldest forms of government. It began in early civilizations in North Africa and Asia where agricultural communities were headed by tribal chiefs. These villages evolved into cities and city-states with large populations. With the rise of these urban centers came monarchies.

The authority of monarchs helped bring order to society. Kings (and, on very rare occasions, queens) commanded armies that protected the resources of the kingdom, particularly land and access to fresh water. Monarchs led battles to build and maintain their kingdom's supremacy. They arranged for public works such as the building of roads, bridges, and temples. And they served as spiritual leaders.

The monarch's subjects included priests, soldiers, administrators, craftsmen, and farmers. The lower classes—the craftsmen and farmers—typically supported ruling classes by paying taxes and tribute to the king.

MESOPOTAMIAN KINGS

Mesopotamia—the land between the Tigris and Euphrates Rivers in today's Iraq—is often referred to as the cradle of civilization. The first city-states that developed in the region were part of the Sumerian civilization. By 3000 BC many of these city-states contained populations of 30,000 to 40,000 people.

Each Sumerian city-state had its own royal dynasty, gods, and temples. Mesopotamian kings, who served as high priests, were believed to rule with divine assistance. They governed for the gods, but generally were not considered to be gods.

An exception to that idea was a Sumerian king named Gilgamesh. The fifth king of Uruk, a city-state located on the Euphrates River, ruled around 2700 BC. His story is told in a poem called the *Epic of Gilgamesh*. In the poem, Gilgamesh is described as part god, and part human. He is also credited with building the great walls that surrounded and protected the city of Uruk. The *Epic of Gilgamesh* is one of the earliest recorded works of literature. It is written in cuneiform, the oldest known written language.

Over the years, the Sumerian city-states fought among themselves for dominance. Around 2300 BC

A portion of the Code of Hammurabi, an ancient collection of laws created by a Mesopotamian king more than 3,700 years ago.

they were conquered by kings of the Akkadian Empire. The founding king of these unified city-states in Mesopotamia was Sargon, who reigned from around 2334 to 2279 BC. He and his descendants introduced the concept of "divine kingship," the idea that the king was a god or a representative of the gods. The empire collapsed around 2100 BC.

Another major power in Mesopotamia was the Babylonian Empire. It originated with the city-state of Babylon, founded in the late third or early second millennium BC on the banks of the Euphrates River.

Writing developed independently in the cities of Mesopotamia, Egypt, China, and Central America. It was first used for recordkeeping, which was essential for monarchs governing large cities. Early writings typically recorded the day-to-day administration of tasks of state, which included running large temples and tracking the movement and storage of goods.

Under King Hammurabi, who ruled from around 1792 to 1750 BC, the city-state expanded into an empire. As king, Hammurabi worked to develop rules of law. He produced the first known written set of laws, known as the Code of Hammurabi. Almost three hundred laws and legal decisions were inscribed on several tall stone pillars, called stelae, for public display in Babylonian cities. They were written in both cuneiform script and in the Akkadian language.

EGYPTIAN PHARAOHS

Around 3000 BC a powerful civilization was also developing in Egypt, where cities had sprung up along the Nile River. This fertile land in North Africa was ruled by pharaohs of 31 different dynasties during the period 3100–30 BC.

According to historical records Menes (also known as Narmer) was the first pharaoh. He is credited with founding the Egyptian Empire by uniting the tribes of Upper and Lower Egypt into one kingdom.

> "WHAT IS THE KING OF UPPER AND LOWER EGYPT? HE IS A GOD BY WHOSE DEALINGS ONE LOVES, THE FATHER AND MOTHER OF ALL MEN, ALONE BY HIM-SELF, WITHOUT AN EQUAL."
>
> —EGYPTIAN HYMN

Egypt saw some of its greatest prosperity during the third through sixth dynasties, which ruled from 2686 to 2125 BC. During that time huge pyramids were built as tombs for the mummified bodies of the pharaohs and queens. The largest pyramid was constructed in Giza for King Khufu around 2540 BC. It covered 13 acres and rose to a height of almost 500 feet. Known today as the Great Pyramid, it stood as a symbol of the power of the Egyptian king.

The pyramids reflected the pharaohs' status in Egyptian society as gods. Egyptian kings were considered divine beings with special powers over natural phenomena. People prayed and made sacrifices to the ruler. Belief in the pharaoh's divinity assured his or her absolute power.

Pharaohs, however, were not supposed to rule by whim. They were to abide by a concept called Ma'at. This was a spiritual principle of truth and justice, and especially of cosmic order and harmony. The pharaoh was regarded as the guardian of Ma'at, responsible for maintaining fundamental order and harmony. In this role, the ruler led important religious ceremonies and built temples to the Egyptian gods.

The Egyptian Empire was at its height from around 1550 to 1070 BC, during the 18th, 19th, and 20th dynasties. At that time the Egyptian state included the Nile Valley from the Nile Delta to today's Sudan, stretching to the east to the borders of the Sinai Peninsula. The empire's efficient bureaucracy and great wealth enabled the continued building of pyramids and monuments, efficient running of its taxation systems, and mobilization of vast armies.

Most pharaohs were men. However, a few women did rule. One was the 18th-dynasty pharaoh Hatshepsut, who reigned for 20 years (1479–1458 BC). She oversaw many public works projects, including a great temple at Deir el Bahri near Thebes (Luxor), which was then the

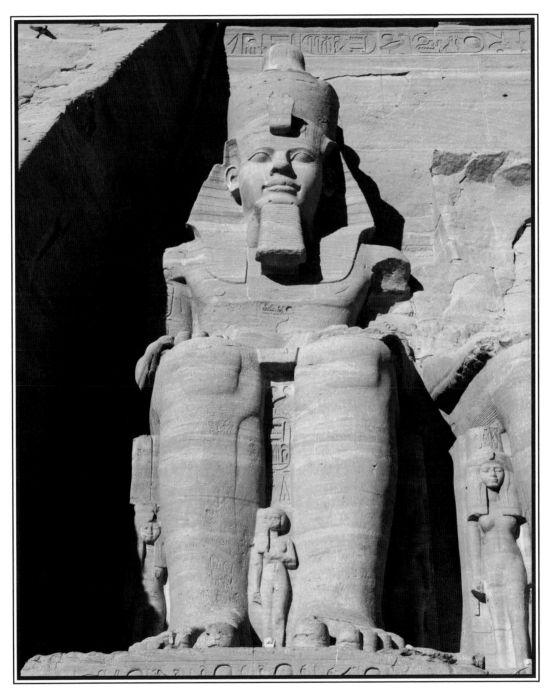

Statue of Pharaoh Ramesses II at a temple in Abu Simbel, Egypt.

capital of Egypt. Famous male pharaohs of the 18th dynasty include Akhenaton and Tutankhamun.

A renowned pharaoh who ruled during Egypt's height was Ramesses II, of the 19th dynasty. During his long reign (ca. 1279–1213 BC), Ramesses conquered lands to the north and south and erected colossal monuments that portrayed him as a strong leader and great pharaoh. Well after his death, he was still worshiped as a god.

Battles against foreign empires would weaken the Egyptian Empire. In 525 BC Egypt was brought under the control of the Achaemenid Empire. It fell to the Macedonian conqueror Alexander the Great in 332 BC. Egypt's 31st and final dynasty would be founded in 305 BC, when one of Alexander's generals, Ptolemy, declared himself pharaoh. The Ptolemaic dynasty gave Egypt its last pharaoh, Cleopatra VII. She killed herself in 30 BC rather than be taken prisoner when Egypt was defeated by Rome.

ACHAEMENID EMPIRE

Centered in today's Iran, the Achaemenid Empire (550–330 BC) reached to Turkey and Egypt in the west and Afghanistan and Pakistan to the east. Sometimes known as the First Persian Empire, it was founded by Cyrus the Great.

Cyrus called himself Shahanshah, or "king of kings." He established an extensive network of roads and an efficient system of administering his far-flung empire. In distant provinces, a governor known as a satrap represented the king's authority. The satrap enforced law, levied taxes, and raised armies. The system enabled the multicultural military power of the Achaemenid Empire to last more than 200 years.

> The first known records of the staff, or scepter, as a symbol of the authority of kings and noblemen can be found in Egyptian hieroglyphs—the stylized pictures used in ancient writing systems.

MACEDONIAN EMPIRE

Ancient Macedonia, located in the northeastern area of modern-day

Greece, became a military power under the rule of Philip II. After Philip's assassination in 336 BC, the king was succeeded by his 20-year-old son, Alexander.

Within 12 years Alexander the Great, as he is known today, had amassed a vast empire. It included Greece, lands of the Persian Empire, Egypt, the Middle East (today's Turkey, Iraq, Syria, and Egypt), and territories that stretched to north-western India. Alexander also assumed the title of Pharaoh of Egypt and King of the Persians (which he took from Darius III, the last king of the Achaemenid Empire).

Alexander claimed to be descended from the mythical Greek hero Heracles. And many of the people his armies conquered considered him a living god. But in 323 BC he showed that he was indeed mortal, dying from an illness or possible poisoning at the age of 32.

One of Alexander's former generals, Lysimachus, went on to rule Thrace (part of the Macedonian

The Macedonian ruler Alexander the Great was the greatest conqueror of the ancient world. At the time of his death in 323 BC, his empire included large portions of southeastern Europe, Egypt, and central Asia.

Empire that is today's Bulgaria, northern Greece, and Turkey). To legitimize his rule, he issued coins that featured Alexander's image. The coins portrayed the great warrior both as a man and as the god Zeus-Amon (a combination of the leading god of the Greeks and the leading god of the Egyptians). The coins were among the first to carry the likeness of a ruler.

ROMAN EMPIRE

According to traditional sources, Rome was founded in 753 BC by twin brothers named Romulus and Remus, with Romulus becoming king after his brother's death in a fraternal dispute. Six kings are said to have followed Romulus. The Roman monarchy, according to tradition, had an unusual feature: kingship wasn't inherited. Rather, kings were elected by members of the senate, an assembly of elders. Kings did serve for life, however. The monarchy is said to have ended in 509 BC, when King Tarquin tried to establish a hereditary dynasty and was overthrown. Scholars aren't certain how much of the traditional account of the Roman monarchy is historically accurate. No written records exist before the mid-fourth century BC—150 years after the supposed reign of Tarquin—and the archaeological evidence from the monarchical period is scant.

The government established by Caesar Augustus, the first Roman emperor, led to a period known as the Pax Romana ("Roman peace"). During this prosperous period from 27 BC to about AD 180, the government of the Roman Empire was stable and the imperial territories were mostly safe from foreign invaders.

In any event, Rome became a republic, headed by two elected consuls. This system of government lasted for about 500 years until a powerful general named Julius Caesar took control of the government as dictator. After his assassination in 44 BC, civil war broke out.

In 31 BC Julius Caesar's grandnephew and heir, Octavian, ended the war by defeating Marc Antony and Cleopatra at the Battle of Actium in Egypt. A few years later, in 27 BC, the Roman senate bestowed on Octavian the honorific title of Augustus

(*August* means "the revered one"). Although he did not carry a scepter or wear a crown, Caesar Augustus assumed the power of an emperor. The Roman senate still existed, but it had little actual authority.

During Augustus's 40-year rule, the Roman Empire enjoyed a period of prosperity and peace. A great deal of construction took place in Rome and around the empire.

> "FOR THE POWER OF THE KING IS MORE THAN HUMAN, AND HIS ARM EXCEEDING LONG."
>
> —HERODOTUS

Like rulers before him, Augustus also made sure his image was before the public eye. Statues of him as a young warrior were erected throughout the empire, and his likeness was stamped on coins. This symbolic presence conveyed the emperor's power and inspired loyalty to Rome. Monarchies that followed would likewise use images and symbols in establishing their authority.

The Roman Empire dominated Europe for several centuries. Its emperors assumed great power. Many of these imperial rulers came to be worshiped as gods.

OLMEC AND MAYAN CIVILIZATIONS

While empires based on monarchy thrived in Asia, Africa, and Europe, they also came into existence in other parts of the world. One was in Central America, where the ancient Olmec civilization emerged around the southern Gulf Coast of Mexico. Often referred to as the mother culture of Central America, the Olmec civilization was the first in the region to build large cities. The culture flourished from around 1400 BC to 400 BC.

Olmec cities were ruled by kings and queens. Like the ancient Egyptians, the Olmecs buried their mummified rulers in pyramids and temple monuments. The Olmecs were an agricultural society. Maize, or corn, was particularly important. Statues of the early kings showed their sacred power by portraying them wearing the ceremonial dress of the maize god.

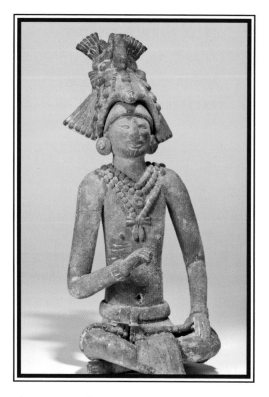

This ceramic figure, which represents a Mayan king, was created around AD 1100. It was found on Jaina Island, a burial site for elite members of Mayan society in the western Yucatan Peninsula.

Another major civilization of Central America was the Mayan culture. The Mayan civilization, which reached its peak between AD 250 and 900, was based in today's southern Mexico, Honduras, Belize, and Guatemala. Tens of thousands of people lived in its huge cities, which like the Olmec urban centers featured pyramids, public monuments, temples, and palaces. Their gods were connected to the natural world. Among the most important were those associated with corn, rain, and the sun.

Mayan monarchs were believed to be descendants of the gods. In religious ceremonies kings and queens performed animal and human sacrifices and bloodletting rites, including self-sacrifice, to try to make contact with the gods or their ancestors. Monarchs made such sacrifices to guarantee good harvests, celebrate victories in war, and ensure order in the world.

THE SHANG AND ZHOU DYNASTIES

A ruler's connection with the gods was also important on the other side of the world, in China. One of the first dynasties of China was the Shang dynasty, whose members ruled for about 500 years, from 1500 to 1050 BC. Their rise to power coincided with the emergence of China's first large cities. Around 1000 BC the Zhou, warriors from the central steppes of Asia, overthrew the Shang dynasty.

The Zhou (ca. 1050–256 BC) were the first Chinese dynasty to establish belief in the Mandate of Heaven. This idea is that the gods approve and support the authority of a just monarch. When that mandate is withdrawn, a ruler loses the right to rule and can be removed. The Shang were defeated, the Zhou claimed, because they no longer held the Mandate of Heaven. The Zhou dynasty spread its empire far beyond the area previously ruled by the Shang. And it thrived longer than any other Chinese dynasty.

KEY IDEA

In many ancient cultures the monarch was believed to connect ordinary people with their gods. Pharaohs and other monarchs identified themselves as gods, deserving of sacrifices and worship in their own right.

Future emperors of China would claim to rule with the gods' blessing, saying they held the Mandate of Heaven. Their governments faced distrust, however, when there were disasters such as floods, famines, or earthquakes. People believed that the gods were offended and the mandate had been withdrawn.

3

MEDIEVAL EMPIRES AND KINGDOMS

During the third century AD, there were two main powers in western Asia and Europe, the Sasanian Empire and the Roman Empire. By the fifth century the western half of the Roman Empire would collapse, and the Eastern Roman Empire would dominate as the Byzantine Empire. At that time, both the Sasanian and Byzantine empires would be matched by a third power in India. These three early empires followed different faiths, and all three were headed by monarchs.

ZORASTRIAN, HINDU, AND CHRISTIAN EMPIRES

A major Persian empire, the Sasanian Empire was a highly centralized state that included today's Iran and Iraq and stretched from modern Syria to Pakistan. Its people followed the Zoroastrian faith, a religion in which twin gods—one good and one evil—engage in a never-ending struggle. The Sasanian kings were considered agents of the good god. Their central role was to impose "divine order" on "demonic chaos." The Sasanian Empire lasted for more than 400 years, from AD 224 to 651.

In northern India, the Gupta Empire was founded in the early fourth century AD and reached its height in the fifth century. The newly revived faith of Hinduism flourished under Gupta rule, as the kings sponsored the building of temples and emphasized their royal connection to the major Hindu deities, such as Vishnu and Shiva. However, the king was not himself considered a god. During the Gupta dynasty, the modern forms of Hinduism in India were established, and the arts and sciences flourished in the empire.

To the west of the Gupta Empire, Emperor Constantine I ruled the Roman Empire between 306 and 337. After converting to Christianity, Constantine began building Christian churches and promoting the Christian faith, which soon became the predominant religion of the Roman Empire.

In the year 395, the Roman Empire split into eastern and western halves, with two separate governments. One government

Constantine I was among the most influential Roman emperors. He emerged from a power struggle in the early fourth century to take complete control over the empire around AD 324. He moved the center of imperial government to a new capital in Asia Minor (modern-day Turkey), which he called Constantinople.

ruled the west from Rome, but in less than a century that part of the empire broke apart into numerous kingdoms ruled by Germanic nobles. The Eastern Roman Empire remained intact and was renamed the Byzantine Empire. Its rulers reigned from the capital city of Constantinople, formerly known as Byzantium. The Christian-based empire included today's Turkey, Greece, the Balkans, and the Middle East.

ISLAMIC CALIPHATES

During the seventh century another new faith, Islam, took hold. It was founded in 622 by the prophet Muhammad. From the Arabian Peninsula, Islam spread quickly—through conquest as well as voluntary conversion— across the Middle East and North Africa following Muhammad's death in 632. However, there was disagreement among followers of Islam, or Muslims, over who should succeed Muhammad as leader of the Muslim community. Eventually this led to the formation of two separate branches of Islam, known as Sunni and Shia.

Islamic leaders were called caliphs. A caliph headed the Muslim political state, or caliphate, and was also considered leader of the *umma*, or community of believers. The first four caliphs were all close companions of Muhammad and were chosen for their piety.

The fifth caliph, Muawiyah, established dynastic rule over the Islamic caliphate. Muawiyah's Umayyad Caliphate lasted from 661 to 750, when it was overthrown by the Abbasids.

From the 8th to 10th centuries, the Abbasid Caliphate stretched from central Asia to Spain. The Abbasid caliphs controlled much of the Middle East and North Africa. Major Muslim cities of the time included Cairo, in Egypt; and Baghdad and Samarra, in Iraq. At different times, both Baghdad and Samarra served as capitals of the empire. Abbasid caliphs built opulent palaces and places of worship, or mosques, in both cities.

TANG DYNASTY

Another major empire of the early medieval world was China's Tang dynasty. Between 500 and 800 the Islamic caliphate and the Tang dynasty

MONGOLIAN EMPIRES

In 1206 Genghis Khan brought together tribes of the central Asian steppes in modern-day Mongolia, and was proclaimed ruler of all Mongols. (*Khan* means "emperor" or "king" in the Mongolian language.) During the 13th and 14th centuries, the renowned warrior-king and his descendants conquered the surrounding lands, creating a vast empire. It reached from eastern Europe to the Sea of Japan, and included large parts of Siberia in the north, the Indian subcontinent to the south, and the Middle East to the west.

Kublai Khan, the grandson of Genghis Khan, conquered China and founded the Yuan dynasty. It controlled China, along with Mongolia, from 1271 to 1368.

dominated the commercial trade of luxury goods throughout Asia and Africa. Such trade was made possible by the Silk Road, a network of roads that at its peak spanned 4,000 miles and connected the East with the Mediterranean world. Among the most valuable items traded were gold, precious stones, spices, and silk.

The Tang dynasty, founded in 618, governed a great civilization of cosmopolitan cities and featured a huge bureaucratic class. Members of the civil service ran various ministries and oversaw public works, the economy, the military, and ceremonial rituals. Two important rulers of the dynasty were military and political leader Emperor Taizong, who reigned from 626 to 649, and Wu Zetian, who ruled from 690 to 705. She was the only woman ever to rule as an emperor in China.

During its mostly peaceful 290-year rule, the Tang dynasty saw a great blossoming of culture and the arts, especially poetry, painting, and calligraphy. There were also a number of significant scientific advances. The empire controlled parts of today's Korea, Manchuria, and northern Vietnam.

JAPANESE MONARCHY

According to Japanese legend, the first Japanese emperor, Jimmu, was the great-grandson of Ninigi. He in turn was the grandson of the Japanese sun goddess Amaterasu. Ninigi supposedly established the throne in 660 BC when Amaterasu made him descend from Heaven to bring peace to the Japanese islands. At that time the goddess gave Ninigi a sacred mirror that would allow him and his successors to speak with her. She also gave him a string of jewels and a sword. The imperial regalia of the mirror, jewels, and sword continue to be used in modern Japanese enthronement ceremonies. The three sacred objects traditionally symbolize the legitimacy and authority of the Japanese emperor.

In 894, during the Fujiwara dynasty (794–1185), Japanese emperors cut off contact and most trade with the rest of the world. Japan would remain isolated for several centuries.

EARLY MIDDLE AGES

In Europe the period from around 500 to 1000 is known as the Early Middle Ages (or, less frequently, the Dark Ages). With the fall of the Western Roman Empire, the stability that the empire had provided was gone. It was a time of violence and unrest, with local rulers battling one another and invasions from tribes such as the Vikings, fierce warriors from Scandinavia.

Ultimately, smaller kingdoms were united into larger ones based on the feudal system. This was a form of governing in which the king owned all the land in his realm, but gave large portions of it to men in exchange for their loyalty and the promise to provide military service.

The men who took the grant of a fiefdom became the king's vassals and were given titles such as duke, earl, viscount,

> "THE JUST AND PEACEFUL KING CAREFULLY THINKS ABOUT EACH CASE, AND NOT DESPISING THE SICK AND POOR OF HIS PEOPLE, SPEAKS JUST JUDGMENTS, PUTTING DOWN THE WICKED AND RAISING THE GOOD."
>
> —MEDIEVAL TREATISE

or baron. The king's vassals also had vassals of their own: they granted other men land in exchange for their allegiance and support. There could be many levels of lords who had vassals committed to them.

While the nobility held their estates on behalf of the monarch, they depended on the peasants, or serfs, to live on and work the land. Farmers had to pay taxes to the lord in the form of livestock or grains. Some serfs worked directly for the lord's family, in the grand house, or manor. By the 1100s the feudal system was in place throughout Europe.

CHARLEMAGNE

Many of the lands of the former Western Roman Empire would be reunited under Charlemagne. Also known as Charles the Great, Charlemagne was the king of the Franks, a Germanic tribe. During his rule, from 768 to 814, he expanded his Frankish kingdom. By the year 800, he had created an empire that included much of western and central Europe. Under the rule of Charlemagne, there was stability and order.

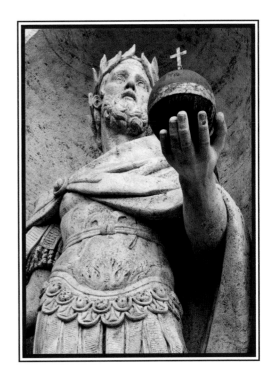

Charlemagne had converted to Christianity, and he worked to bring the faith to the lands he conquered. On Christmas Day in the year 800, Pope Leo III crowned Charlemagne, proclaiming him emperor of the Romans.

The association of political power with the spiritual authority of the Catholic Church would be very important in the Middle Ages. Around Charlemagne's time, coronation ceremonies in kingdoms and

During the years he ruled western Europe, Charlemagne promoted learning and established an effective system of government.

empires that had converted to Christianity began to include the religious ritual of anointment with holy chrism. (Chrism is a mixture of oil and aromatic resins.) The anointment symbolized sanctification or blessing, and it affirmed the king's role as a spiritual as well as a worldly leader. Anointment also implied that the right to rule came from God.

Charlemagne's empire didn't survive intact for very long after his death in 814. The empire was officially divided into three kingdoms, each ruled by one of Charlemagne's grandsons, in 843. By the end of the century, these kingdoms had disintegrated into multiple smaller states.

ANGLO-SAXONS

Germanic tribes invaded Britain during the early Middle Ages. These tribes included the Angles, Saxons, and Jutes, who formed kingdoms headed by monarchs. Between 500 and 850, seven Anglo-Saxon kingdoms controlled southern, central, and eastern Britain: East Anglia, Essex, Kent, Mercia, Northumbria, Sussex, and Wessex.

One of the most renowned Anglo-Saxon kings was Alfred of Wessex, known as Alfred the Great. During his rule (871–899), Alfred organized a system of laws. He also successfully defended Wessex from Viking invaders.

Other Anglo-Saxon kingdoms didn't fare as well in the face of attacks by the Norse warriors. By 900 Vikings held lands in the north and east of Britain. Wessex claimed lands in the south and west.

In 927 King Athelstan of Wessex, the grandson of Alfred the Great, defeated the Vikings. He set about building a unified kingdom of England, assuming the title King of All Britain. It was the first time the region was united, although the union did not last.

Early Norman kings of England were vassals to the king of France. Many spoke only French, while their subjects spoke Old English, the language of the Anglo-Saxons.

A UNITED ENGLAND

England would ultimately be united by William the Conqueror, a warrior from a region of northern France

This detail from the Bayeux Tapestry, an embroidered cloth made during the 11th century, shows King Harold II of England feasting in London with nobles who had supported his claim to the throne in early 1066. In the feudal system, noblemen promised to be loyal to the king and provide financial and military support. In turn the king gave these nobles, called vassals, property and promised to protect their rights.

known as Normandy. In October 1066 he defeated the soldiers of the Anglo-Saxon king Harold. The following December, a coronation ceremony held in Westminster Abbey legitimized William as king of England.

During his reign as William I (1066–1087), the Norman king combined Anglo-Saxon and Norman laws, customs, and institutions. He granted parcels of land to his knights and had them swear loyalty to him, thus introducing the feudal system to England. This allowed him to establish a strong centralized monarchy. (Such oaths of loyalty remain part of the British coronation service.)

For monarchs to stay in power, they needed the advice and support of the most powerful of their subjects—the nobility and senior clergy. William consulted with his vassals at meetings he convened known as Great Councils. Later English kings would include members of the clergy, such as bishops and abbots. Around the 1230s these councils became known as Parliament. The name came from the Old French word *parlement*, which means "speaking."

Other English kings would also introduce changes to strengthen the monarchy. Henry II ruled from 1154 to 1189. During his reign he expanded the power of the royal courts by increasing the number of criminal cases tried in the king's court and transferring property cases from local courts to royal courts. These actions increased the amount of money that the monarch controlled. And raising money was often a concern of medieval kings.

Henry II's son was Richard I, who ruled from 1189 to 1199. A gifted military leader, he spent most of his time on the battlefield. Known as Richard the Lionheart, he fought in France for land claimed by England. And he led armed expeditions to present-day Israel and Palestine as part of the Crusades. The Crusades were a series of conflicts that took place from 1095 to 1272 as the Christian countries of Europe and the Byzantine Empire fought to win back the Holy Land from the Islamic caliphates.

During the 1100s and 1200s, the Ayyubid Caliphate ruled much of the Middle East. Richard fought against its founder, a great warrior known as Saladin. While Richard was away from England, his brother John claimed the throne, becoming king in 1199.

THE MAGNA CARTA

"[H]ERE IS A LAW WHICH IS ABOVE THE KING AND WHICH EVEN HE MUST NOT BREAK. THIS REAFFIRMATION OF A SUPREME LAW AND ITS EXPRESSION IN A GENERAL CHARTER IS THE GREAT WORK OF MAGNA CARTA; AND THIS ALONE JUSTIFIES THE RESPECT IN WHICH MEN HAVE HELD IT."

—WINSTON CHURCHILL, 1955

King John was an unpopular ruler. And his popularity decreased as the expenses incurred by conflicts with France forced him to raise taxes. After losing lands to France, John returned from battle to England in need of money. But when he demanded that his feudal barons pay an extra tax without their consent, they rebelled. In 1215 civil war broke out, and the barons confronted King John on the battlefield and forced him to sign the Magna Carta.

This legal document guaranteed certain basic rights and other liberties for all free men in the kingdom. It limited

Rebellious English barons watch King John sign the Magna Carta.

the monarch's ability to raise funds. And it was the first formal document stating that the monarch was under the same rule of law as his people. John would later say he signed the Magna Carta under duress, and he refused to abide by the document. But he died soon after, in 1216, and was succeeded by his son, Henry III.

John's grandson, Edward I, whose reign began in 1272, carried on the traditions of fighting wars. Among the battles he fought in were the uprisings led by Scottish leaders William Wallace and Robert the Bruce. But he was determined to unite England, Wales, and Scotland under his rule by force. Meanwhile, the role of Parliament in the government increased. To raise taxes to pay his armies, Edward had to convene Parliament. Because of the Magna Carta, Parliament—and not the monarch—had the authority to make legislation levying taxes.

The German king Otto III is crowned Holy Roman Emperor in Rome, 996. His grandfather, Otto the Great, and father, Otto II, had previously held this title.

4

EARLY MODERN EMPIRES

During medieval times the power of the Roman Catholic Church grew in western Europe. Based in Rome, the pope, as the Church's official leader, claimed authority over all Christians in Europe. This meant the pope had greater power than a king. Many monarchs did not agree. They believed their divine right to be king justified their right to final authority.

THE HOLY ROMAN EMPIRE

Church authority was affirmed when Pope Leo III crowned Charlemagne in 800. But Charlemagne's empire broke apart in the decades after his death.

In the 960s Otto the Great, ruler of the kingdom of Germany, gained control of the kingdoms of Burgundy (in France) and Italy. He established a church-state alliance that reunited a portion of

Charlemagne's empire, which became the Holy Roman Empire. In 962 Pope John XII crowned Otto as its emperor.

The Holy Roman Empire would last for several centuries. However, it was not a hereditary monarchy. Princes of Germanic kingdoms, or electors, selected the ruler of the German kingdom. And that person would be crowned by the pope as emperor.

Concern that popes were interfering in the selection of German kings led one of the emperors, Charles IV, to call for the passage of the Golden Bull of 1356. This legal decree by the Imperial Diet (an assembly of the Imperial Estates of the Holy Roman Empire) established details of the election process and specified the electors. Charles sponsored passage of the legal decree as a way to assert monarchal authority in German politics over the authority of the pope.

THE PROTESTANT REFORMATION

Emperors and kings were not alone is their disagreement with the policies of the Roman Catholic Church. In 1517 an Augustinian monk named Martin Luther protested Church practices by nailing a list of his grievances on the door of a Catholic cathedral in Wittenberg, Germany. That act led to religious division among Christians. In a movement known as the Reformation, Protestants separated from the Roman Catholic Church. They rejected the pope's claim to supreme authority in religious and political matters and created a separate branch of Christianity.

The Reformation movement caused religious and political turmoil throughout Europe. During his reign from 1519 to 1556 the Holy Roman Emperor Charles V fought in religious wars that swept the continent. He struggled to hold the empire together as European kingdoms accepted Protestantism. At the same time he was also dealing with Turkish forces of the Ottoman

> The last Byzantine emperor was Constantine XI. He died in 1453, while fighting to defend Constantinople from Muslim armies led by the Ottoman sultan Mehmed II.

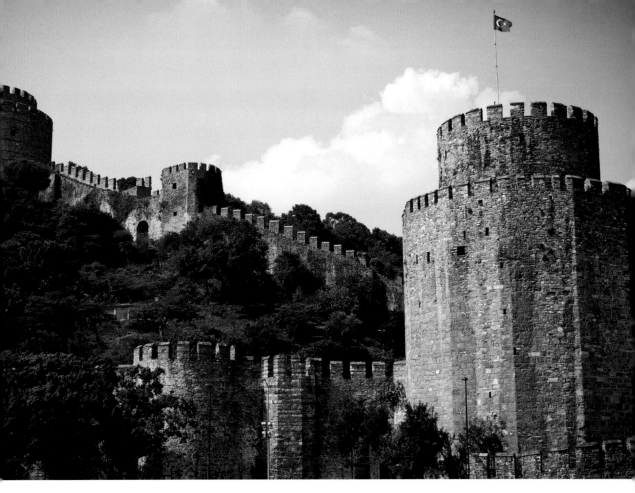

The Ottoman sultans constructed fortresses like this one to control the Bosporus strait, a key waterway near their capital at Istanbul (formerly Constantinople).

Empire, which were attacking the Christian lands of the former Byzantine Empire in the east.

OTTOMAN EMPIRE

As Christianity grew in western Europe, the Middle East saw the rise of another Islamic empire. Osman I was a Turkish leader from a kingdom in the northwestern Anatolia region of today's Turkey. In 1299 he declared his emirate's independence, thus founding the Ottoman dynasty. (An emirate is a kingdom headed by a Muslim ruler.) The Islamic leader quickly amassed an empire by conquering lands formerly controlled by the Christian Byzantine Empire.

THE SAFAVID EMPIRE

A rival to the Ottoman Empire was the unified Iranian state known as the Safavid Empire. Founded in 1502, it eventually included the lands of modern Iran and Iraq, as well as parts of Turkey and Georgia. One of the most famous Safavid rulers was Shah Abbas I the Great, who reigned from 1587 to 1629. He opened up Persia to trade with western European nations, centralized the government, improved the civil service, and modernized the army. Under the Safavid rulers, Shia Islam was established as the region's official religion.

As the Ottoman Empire continued to spread in the 1300s, its leaders assumed the title of sultan. The disciplined fighting forces of the Ottoman Empire ensured its rise as a superpower. Ottoman Turks conquered Constantinople and brought an end to the Byzantine Empire. Renamed Istanbul, the city became the new capital of the Ottoman Empire.

One of the most powerful Ottoman sultans was Suleiman I, whose reign began in 1520. By the time of his death 46 years later, the empire controlled North Africa and the eastern Mediterranean. This forced western Europeans to find trade routes by sea.

Suleiman developed and established new laws and created an efficient civil service. The sultan, who lived at the same time as the English king Henry VIII and the Holy Roman Emperor Charles V, was known to Europeans as Suleiman the Magnificent.

A CHANGING WORLD

A modern world was emerging by the 1600s. In Europe, advancement in the fields of arts, literature, science, and philosophy were part of a period that became known as the Renaissance.

It was also a time of exploration, as the rulers of the kingdoms of Portugal and Spain funded major oceangoing expeditions. In Spain the monarchy funded the voyage of Christopher Columbus in 1492. The young Spanish king Charles I, who was also the Holy Roman emperor Charles V, sponsored ships led by Ferdinand Magellan in 1519 as they circumnavigated the globe for the first time. The 1500s and 1600s saw vast exploration by Portuguese and Spanish sailors.

Reports about unknown lands helped foster a new age of learning for the Western world. And that learning was advanced by the development of technologies such as the printing press. Access to the written word

During the 16th century, the New World conquests of Spanish soldiers like Hernán Cortés, Francisco Pizarro, and Hernando de Soto, and the adventures of explorers like Ferdinand Magellan and Juan Cabrillo, helped make Spain's King Charles I the wealthiest ruler in Europe. (As Holy Roman Emperor, he was known as Charles V.)

INCAS AND AZTECS

In 1500 the Inca Empire was the largest in the world. More than 12 million people were part of the empire, which included today's Colombia, Chile, and other parts of western South America. Its capital city was Cusco, in today's Peru. The Incas raised food using irrigation projects and canals; in a region with mountainous terrain, crops grew on terraced fields. The civilization was a highly organized society with an extensive road network, abundant food, and a powerful military force.

Around the same time in Central America, another indigenous civilization was also flourishing. At its height in the early 1500s it stretched from today's southern Mexico to Guatemala, from the Atlantic Ocean to the Pacific. The Aztec civilization consisted mostly of city-states ruled by individual kings. Many of these cities featured pyramids, temples, and paved roads. Kings paid tribute to the Aztec emperor, in the form of cloth, jewelry, corn, or gold.

Spanish conquerors destroyed both the Aztec and Inca Empires. The Aztecs were defeated in 1521, the Incas in 1533.

encouraged a rise of literacy. As people became more informed, some of them questioned the role of the Catholic Church and the monarchy in their lives.

ENGLAND'S TUDOR KINGS

In the 15th century, rival branches of England's royal family—the House of Lancaster and the House of York—fought a series of conflicts for the throne. In 1485 Henry VII of the House of Lancaster brought the 30-year-long Wars of the Roses to an end by defeating his rival, Richard III of the House of York. Henry assumed the throne as the founder of the Tudor dynasty. His court promoted the ideas and learning of the Renaissance. And as monarch he assumed greater control over the country's administration and coffers. His shrewd accounting practices ensured that the monarchy was adequately funded.

The religious division due to the Reformation peaked in England during the time of King Henry VIII, who reigned from 1509 to 1547. In his desire to divorce his queen, Catherine of Aragon, he broke away from the Roman Catholic Church. He dissolved Catholic monasteries in the country and seized their property. And he established the Church of England and declared himself its head, thus making him both a political and religious ruler.

Henry claimed that he ruled with the approval of God. He maintained the title of *Fidei Defensor*, or Defender of the Faith, first bestowed on him by the pope. But he no longer defended the Roman Catholic Church. Instead the title represented the role of the English monarch as defender of the Church of England.

After Henry's death in 1547 all three of his children would assume the throne. Edward VI died within a few years, and his sister Mary I succeeded

Queen Elizabeth I, last of the Tudor monarchs, was one of the most popular rulers in England's history. During her long reign, England asserted itself as an international economic and military power.

him. A devout Catholic, she and her husband, Philip II of Spain, persecuted Protestants, causing religious turmoil throughout England. After Mary's death in 1558 Elizabeth, who was Protestant, ascended the throne.

Elizabeth's 45-year reign would become known as the Golden Age of England. During this time William Shakespeare wrote his famous plays and Sir Francis Drake explored the New World. After the British navy defeated the powerful Spanish Armada in 1588, the world viewed the nation with respect. In a speech before the troops defending the land, Elizabeth I affirmed her dedication to her country, saying, "I know I have but the body of a weak and feeble woman; but I have the heart of a king, and of a king of England too."

ENGLAND'S CONSTITUTIONAL MONARCHY

After Elizabeth's death in 1603, King James VI of Scotland succeeded to the throne, ruling over both England and Scotland. His son Charles I, who became king in 1625, would bring the country to civil war.

Charles believed that his was an absolute monarchy. Instead of working with Parliament, as previous kings had

IN A SPEECH TO ENGLAND'S PARLIAMENT IN 1609, KING JAMES I EXPLAINED HIS BELIEF IN THE POWER OF THE MONARCHY.
"KINGS ARE JUSTLY CALLED GODS, FOR THAT THEY EXERCISE A MANNER OR RESEMBLANCE OF DIVINE POWER UPON EARTH," THE KING SAID. "GOD HATH POWER TO CREATE OR DESTROY, MAKE OR UNMAKE AT HIS PLEASURE, TO GIVE LIFE, OR SEND DEATH, TO JUDGE ALL, AND TO BE JUDGED NOR ACCOUNTABLE TO NONE. . . . AND THE LIKE POWER HAVE KINGS: THEY MAKE AND UNMAKE THEIR SUBJECTS, THEY HAVE POWER OF RAISING, AND CASTING DOWN, OF LIFE AND OF DEATH, JUDGES OVER ALL THEIR SUBJECTS, AN DIN ALL CAUSES, AND YET ACCOUNTABLE TO NONE BUT GOD ONLY."

done, he fought against it. In 1629 he dissolved the legislative body. He did not call Parliament into session again until 1640. Their conflicts over taxation and control of the military led in 1642 to the English Civil War, between Royalists and Parliamentarians. After losing the war, Charles I was tried, found guilty of treason, and beheaded in 1649. He was the first British monarch to be executed for treason.

The British monarchy was abolished, and a Council of State headed by Oliver Cromwell was set up. But the new government did not last. Eleven years later, in 1660, Parliament restored the monarchy.

In 1689 Parliament asserted authority over King William III and Queen Mary II when it passed the Bill of Rights. The set of laws regulated the relationship between the monarch and the people. It limited powers of the king and guaranteed rights of Parliament, including freedom of speech, the requirement to hold regular elections, and the right to petition the monarch without fear of retribution. The Bill of Rights also required that the Crown seek the consent of the people, as represented in Parliament. The document essentially made Britain a constitutional monarchy.

England and Scotland merged into one kingdom in 1707, and the country became known as Great Britain. Its first prime minister, Robert Walpole, came to power in 1721.

DIVINE KINGS

The beheaded king, Charles I, was one of many medieval monarchs in England and France who believed that divine

> "[KINGS ARE] GOD'S ANOINTED, NOT IN RESPECT OF THE OIL WHICH THE BISHOP USETH, BUT IN CONSIDERATION OF THEIR POWER, WHICH IS ORDAINED, OF THEIR SWORD, WHICH IS AUTHORIZED, OF THEIR PERSONS, WHICH RE ELECTED BY GOD, AND INDUED WITH THE GIFTS OF HIS SPIRIT FOR THE BETTER RULING AND GUIDING OF HIS PEOPLE."
>
> —ARCHBISHOP CRANMER TO EDWARD VI, 1547

Monarchs secured money for their treasuries by conquering other countries and demanding tribute, by taxing their subjects, and by selling offices or crown lands.

authority from God gave them the ability to heal the sick with their touch. They believed they could cure people stricken with the disease known as scrofula, or the King's Evil, by placing their hands around the swellings caused by the infection. Kings and queens arranged meetings with hundreds of afflicted people at a time in order to "heal" them with a royal touch. Some of these rulers included the English monarchs Charles I and Queen Anne, who came to the throne in 1702. French kings continued the practice until as late as 1825.

ABSOLUTE MONARCHIES

Although absolute monarchy did not take hold in Great Britain, it succeeded in other European countries during the 17th and 18th centuries. This was particularly true in France, Spain, Prussia, and Austria. The monarchs of these states ruled autocratically, holding supreme rule in both lawmaking and policymaking. Rulers continued to justify this power as their divine right. They and many of their subjects believed that God had chosen them to serve the land.

King Louis XIV of France, who reigned from 1643 to 1715, best exemplified an absolute ruler. During his reign he weakened the power of the nobles, while increasing his own authority. He justified his rule by saying, "L'état, c'est mois," or "I am the state." The king paid little attention to the needs of his nation's people. Instead he lived extravagantly, spending exorbitant amounts of money on his royal court in Versailles, outside Paris.

5

DECLINE OF MONARCHY

During the late 1600s and 1700s Europe saw the rise of an intellectual movement known as the Enlightenment. It emphasized reason, the scientific method, and individualism. As a result of this new thinking, some people questioned the role of monarchs in their lives.

REJECTING RULERS

Many people wanted a say in their government. In the British colonies of North America, people refused to accept King George III as their king by divine right. In 1776 they declared independence, forming the United States of America.

In 1789 in France, workers and the poor took action to improve their lives. They formed a National Assembly, which passed the Declaration of the Rights of Man and of the Citizen. This

A crowd watches a nobleman being executed on the guillotine during the French Revolution, 1790s.

document stated that all people "are born and remain free and equal in rights." No one—not even the king—could take away these rights. In the years that followed, France experienced political upheaval and violence. Many members of the aristocracy were beheaded. Eventually the monarchy was abolished and, in 1793, King Louis XVI and his wife, Queen Marie Antoinette, were executed.

ENLIGHTENED MONARCHS

Some rulers welcomed leaders of the Enlightenment into their courts and were inspired to institute reforms in their government. One of them was the king of Prussia, Frederick II, who reigned from 1740 to 1786. He became famous for establishing bureaucratic reforms that made the Prussian civil service more efficient, and for codifying the law. Also known as Frederick the Great, the Prussian king referred to himself as "the first servant of the state."

Other enlightened monarchs typically allowed religious toleration, freedom of speech and the press, and the right to hold private property. They worked to build stronger nations by reforming laws. Most of these monarchs, who included Catherine II of Russia and Carlos III of Spain, developed programs to advance education, science, and the arts.

ROYAL RELATIONS

In the late 1700s, Britain was an industrial and military power. At the same time, its military might, particularly its naval strength, led to the growth of an empire. By the late 1800s the British Empire controlled much of the globe, from Iraq to India, from large parts of Africa to Australia. Queen Victoria, who succeeded to the throne in June 1837, ruled the British Empire at its peak.

In 1840 Victoria married a prince of two dukedoms in Germany, Albert of Saxe-Coburg-Gotha. They would have nine children, many of whom married into other royal families of Europe. The queen ruled until January 1901, a span of more than 63 years.

Victoria is sometimes called the grandmother of Europe. At the turn of the 20th century her son King Edward VII was the uncle of the German emperor Kaiser Wilhelm II; Tsar Nicholas II of Russia; King Alfonso XIII of Spain; and Carl Eduard, Duke of Saxe-Coburg-Gotha. The British king was brother-in-law to George I of the Hellenes (the king of Greece) and King Frederick VIII of Denmark. And

The period in which Queen Victoria ruled Great Britain, from 1837 to 1901, is known as the Victorian era.

> Queen Victoria's grandson George V succeeded to the British throne in 1910. Seven years later, while Britain was fighting Germany in World War I, George changed his German-sounding family name—Saxe-Coburg-Gotha—to Windsor.

Edward was cousin to the kings of Belgium, Portugal, and Bulgaria, and to the queen of the Netherlands.

WORLD WAR I

After sitting on the British throne for just nine years, Edward VII died in 1910. His son George V succeeded him.

Four years later, in 1914, the heir to the Austro-Hungarian Empire was murdered at Sarajevo by a Serbian nationalist. The assassination of Archduke Franz Ferdinand led to a huge conflict that engulfed Europe.

On one side of the war were the Central Powers: Germany, the Austro-Hungarian Empire, the Ottoman Empire, and the Kingdom of Bulgaria. They were opposed by the Allies, including Great Britain, France, Russia, and later the United States. The Great War, later known as World War I, would last until 1918 and claim the lives of more than 10 million soldiers.

The Central Powers suffered defeat, and they paid the price with the loss of their monarchies. In 1918 Germany's Kaiser Wilhelm II was forced to abdicate, and the monarchy was abolished. That same year saw the end of the monarchy of the Austro-Hungarian Empire when Emperor Karl I was deposed.

Other monarchies fell as a direct or indirect result of World War I. Russia's Tsar Nicholas had been forced to abdicate in 1917, and he and his family were murdered the following year. In 1922 Sultan Mehmed VI was forced from power and the Ottoman sultanate abolished. The Greek monarchy was abolished in 1924 (although it would be restored in 1935.)

WORLD WAR II

The Second World War, which began in 1939, would alter monarchies in Japan and Italy. The two countries, along with Germany, formed the Axis, which fought the Allies (principally Great Britain, France, the Soviet Union, and the United States). When World War II ended in 1945, one monarchy would be abolished and the other greatly diminished.

In Italy a constitutional monarchy had been established, under the royal House of Savoy, in 1861. During the 1920s, however, King Victor Emmanuel III had allowed Benito Mussolini to eliminate Italy's democratic institutions and create a fascist dictatorship. In June 1946, after their country's defeat in World War II, Italian citizens held a popular referendum in which they voted to abolish the monarchy. Italy became a republic.

In the 19th century, during a period of political upheaval known as the Meiji Restoration, Japan had reestablished its monarchy, with the emperor as absolute ruler. As in the past, the emperor claimed divine ancestry. Emperor Meiji, who ruled from 1867 to 1912, and his sons were regarded as god-kings.

This belief in the divine emperor still held when the

Nicholas II, the last tsar of Russia, with his oldest son Alexei, the heir apparent, circa 1914. A 1917 revolution in Russia forced Nicholas II to give up the throne, and he was imprisoned with his family. In 1918 they were executed, ending the Romanov dynasty of Russian tsars.

The oldest monarchy in Europe is in Denmark. It was established in the early 10th century by Gorm the Old, a warrior chief who unified clans into the kingdom of Denmark. Denmark became a constitutional monarchy in 1849.

grandson of Meiji, Emperor Hirohito, held the throne during World War II. After Japan's defeat in 1945, the monarchy was not dissolved. But the emperor was forced to renounce the idea that Japan's imperial rulers were gods. And he had to accept his role as laid out in a new constitution—that the emperor was only a symbolic leader, with no political power.

THE COMMONWEALTH

The British monarchy continued after World War II. But the British Empire decreased dramatically in size as its many colonies, protectorates, and territories became independent. During the reign of King George VI, who ruled from 1936 to 1952, India and Pakistan gained independence. Upon his death Elizabeth II ascended to the throne. In the years that followed, new countries emerged from British lands in Asia (such as Sri Lanka), Africa (including Ghana, Kenya, and Nigeria), and the Caribbean (such as Trinidad and Tobago). Many of these independent countries joined the Commonwealth of Nations, an intergovernmental organization mostly made up of former colonies of the British Empire. Queen Elizabeth serves as its ceremonial head.

In addition to ruling the United Kingdom, Elizabeth II is also monarch and head of state of 15 parliamentary democracies that remain as Commonwealth realms. They include Australia, Belize, Canada, Jamaica, and New Zealand.

ROYAL EQUALITY

During the second half of the 20th century, several monarchies in Europe opened the door for women. The first-born child, regardless of gender, would legally have the right to the throne.

For centuries European monarchies abided by Salic law, which prohibited females and descendants in the female line from inheriting land, titles, and offices. In 1953 the constitution in Denmark was revised to allow a woman to ascend to the throne. In 1980 Sweden became the first European monarchy to declare equal primogeniture. This means that the crown goes to the eldest child, regardless of gender. The Netherlands, Norway, and Belgium followed suit. And in October 2011 all 16 countries that are realms of the British Commonwealth approved similar reform in royal succession.

MONARCHIES IN ASIA

Like Japan, the countries of Cambodia, Bhutan, and Thailand (formerly known as Siam) have hereditary monarchies. They are also constitutional monarchies. The Kingdom of Cambodia is a restored monarchy that was reinstated in 1993 within a multiparty democracy. The Himalayan nation of Bhutan became a constitutional monarchy in 2008, when King Jigme Khesar Namgyel Wangchuck ratified a constitution transferring much of his power to the Council of Cabinet Ministers.

The ancient absolute monarchy of Siam, founded in 1350, became a constitutional one in 1932 after a bloodless military coup. In December 2010 its king, Bhumibol Adulyadej, who took the throne in 1946, was recognized as the world's longest-reigning monarch. Most Thais regard their king with reverence, and strict rules prohibit anyone from criticizing him. Prison sentences of three to five years have been given for insulting the king, queen, or heir to the throne.

Malaysia is considered a federal parliamentary democracy with a constitutional monarch. Hereditary monarchs, or sultans, govern 9 of the 13 states that make up the federation of Malaysia. The sultans select a king, or "Paramount Ruler," who serves a five-year term as ceremonial head of state.

Nearby Brunei is an absolute monarchy. Its 1959 constitution established the sultan as the head of state with full executive authority. The same family has ruled the sultanate, officially named the Malay Islamic Monarchy, for more than six centuries. Hassanal Bolkiah has ruled the country since 1967.

King Bhumibol Adulyadej of Thailand (right) meets with UN Secretary-General Kofi Annan at the royal residence in Hua Hin, 2006.

MONARCHIES IN THE MIDDLE EAST

A few Middle Eastern countries are constitutional monarchies. But their rulers are not ceremonial figureheads. The leaders of Bahrain, Jordan, and Kuwait tend to hold greater powers than constitutional monarchs do in most other parts of the world.

For example, in Jordan the king has real political power. He appoints the country's prime minister and cabinet and can dissolve Parliament. Members of the Hashemite family have sat on the throne since the 1921 founding of the Emirate of Transjordan, a British protectorate. In 1946 Transjordan gained independence from Britain was renamed the Hashemite Kingdom of Jordan. The royal family claims to being descended from the Arab chieftain Quraysh, who was a descendant of the prophet Muhammad. Thus, the Hashemites claim direct descent from the founder of Islam. King Abdullah II has reigned in Jordan since 1999.

In the constitutional emirate of Kuwait the amir (an alternate spelling of emir) serves both as the head of state and the head of government. He has the last word on government policies. He also has the power to dissolve the National Assembly, although the constitution requires that new elections be held within 60 days. Kuwait has been under the rule of the Al Sabah family since the mid-18th century.

In countries with absolute monarchies, the rulers typically serve as both head of state and government leader. In Oman, for example, Sultan Qaboos is both sultan and prime minister. (He also heads the foreign, defense, and finance ministries of the government.) In Saudi Arabia the king is the chief of state and head of government.

The Kingdom of Saudi Arabia is named after the ruling Al Saud family. King Abdul-Aziz established Saudi Arabia in 1932. Following his death in 1953, he has been succeeded by his sons. (In Saudia Arabia the throne usually passes to the monarch's next eldest brother.) Abdullah bin Abdul-Aziz Al Saud succeeded his half-brother King Fahd, in August 2005. Abdullah had governed as regent since 1998, when Fahd suffered a debilitating stroke.

Another absolute monarchy is Qatar, an emirate that has been ruled by the Al Thani family since the mid-1800s. In 1995 Crown Prince Hamad bin Khalifa deposed his father to become emir. He subsequently introduced many reforms, including a constitution providing for a Shura (consultative) council. In late 2011 Sheikh Hamad announced that Qatar would hold its first national elections, in 2013.

Abdullah bin Abdul-Aziz Al Saud has been king of Saudi Arabia since 2005.

During the traditional Islamic investiture ceremony, Saudi kings receive an oath of allegiance, or *bay'ah*, from tribal chiefs, Islamic clerics, and other prominent Saudis. In 2005, when Abdullah officially became king, hundreds performed the ceremony. Each person shook hands with Abdullah while saying, "I express my allegiance to you. I hear and obey, except in what would disobey God."

ARAB SPRING UPRISINGS

In early 2011 civil unrest shook the Arab world. Hundreds of thousands of people took part in rallies and protests in an effort to bring about political reform. This movement in several countries of North Africa and the Middle East has been referred to as the "Arab Spring."

In countries with monarchies, demonstrators called on leaders to make constitutional reforms. Among their demands were calls for limits on the monarch's authority and increases in the powers of elected legislatures. The protests led some kings to promise certain political reforms. In June 2011 King Abdullah of Jordan pledged that future governments would be elected, not appointed, but he did not say when such elections would be held. In January 2012 King Hamad of Bahrain proposed constitutional amendments that would strengthen the parliament and limit the powers of the royal family.

The power of the monarchy remains strong in several countries of the Middle East. But the Arab uprisings present the potential to bring about change.

USEFULNESS OF THE MONARCHY

At the turn of the 20th century, monarchy was the most common form of government. Today most governments are republics. There are fewer than 50 monarchal governments. And most of them are constitutional ones.

Critics of monarchy call it a relic that is no longer relevant in modern times. They complain that figurehead rulers of constitutional monarchies cannot accomplish much because they have no real political power.

Although Jordan has a constitutional monarchy, King Abdullah II still holds considerable power in the country's government.

Supporters counter that members of royal families often play important ambassadorial and ceremonial roles in government. And they often do good, by supporting or serving as spokespersons for charitable groups.

In Britain, the monarchy has many fans. The interest and celebration over the 2011 wedding of Prince William and Kate Middleton showed that the British monarchy continues to make a powerful and direct connection with the people of the United Kingdom. A poll taken at the time found that 70 percent of Britons supported keeping the monarchy.

Many citizens have great faith in the institution, and consider it part of their identity. When asked whether the monarchy was necessary, one woman told the *Christian Science Monitor*, "The queen will hold things together. I can't imagine England without a monarchy, it wouldn't be England anymore!"

CHAPTER NOTES

p. 18:   "What is the king . . ." Angela Thomas, *Egyptian Gods and Myths* (London: Shire Publications, 2001), p. 25.

p. 23:   "For the power of . . ." Henry Cary, trans., *Herodotus* (London: George Bell & Sons, 1901), p. 542.

p. 30:   "The just and peaceful . . ." Neil MacGregor, *A History of the World in 100 Objects* (New York: Viking, 2011), p. 344.

p. 34:   "[H]ere is a law . . ." Henry Steele Commager, ed., *Churchill's History of the English-Speaking Peoples* (New York: Barnes & Noble Books, 1994), p. 58.

p. 44:   "I know I have . . ." Modern History Sourcebook, "Queen Elizabeth I: Against the Spanish Armada, 1588." http://www.fordham.edu/halsall/mod/1588elizabeth.asp

p. 44:   "Kings are justly called gods . . ." Suzanne McIntire and William E. Burns, *Speeches in World History* (New York: Facts on File, 2009), p. 137.

p. 45:   "[Kings are] God's anointed . . ." John Edmund Cox, ed., *Miscellaneous Writings and Letters of Thomas Cranmer* (Vancouver, B.C., Canada: Regent College Publishing, 2001), p. 126.

p. 48:   "are born and remain . . ." The Avalon Project, "Declaration of the Rights of Man—1789." http://avalon.law.yale.edu/18th_century/rightsof.asp

p. 56:   "I express my . . ." "Clerics, Chiefs Pledge Loyalty to New Saudi King," msnbc.com, August 3, 2005. http://www.msnbc.msn.com/id/8793922/ns/world_news-mideast_n_africa/t/clerics-chiefs-pledge-loyalty-new-saudi-king/#.T0Zzx5jN6kI

p. 57:   "The queen will hold . . ." Robert Marquand, "As William and Kate Await Honeymoon, Britain's Monarchy Enjoys Its Own," *Christian Science Monitor* (May 6, 2011).

CHRONOLOGY

CA. 4000 BC: Monarchy emerges as a form of government in large urban civilizations.

CA. 3500 BC: Egypt is united, forming a kingdom ruled by pharaohs.

CA. 2540 BC: King Khufu builds the Great Pyramid as a symbol of the power and divine rule of Egyptian kings.

CA. 1780 BC: In Mesopotamia, King Hammurabi establishes and publicizes a code of laws.

CA. 550 BC: Cyrus the Great founds the Achaemenid Empire.

30 BC: The last pharaoh of Egypt, Cleopatra, dies.

800:   Charlemagne is crowned king of what will later become the Holy Roman Empire.

1066:   William of Normandy defeats the Anglo-Saxons in England.

1215:   Rebellious barons force King John of England to sign the Magna Carta, a document establishing that the king is not above the rule of law.

1517:   Beginning of Protestant Reformation in Europe, which creates religious and political unrest.

1689:   British Parliament passes the Bill of Rights, which establishes a constitutional monarchy in England.

1789:   Beginning of the French Revolution, which will eventually lead to the abolishment of France's monarchy.

1914–18: World War I, which directly or indirectly leads to the abolishment of monarchies in Germany, Russia, Austria-Hungary, and other countries.

1945:   With the end of World War II the Japanese emperor is forced to accept a symbolic role in a constitutional monarchy. In Italy, the monarchy is abolished the following year.

1952:   Queen Elizabeth II ascends the British throne following the death of her father, George VI.

2012:   Arab Spring protests pressure monarchs in Bahrain, Jordan, and other Middle East nations to make political reforms.

GLOSSARY

ABDICATE—to renounce one's claim to the throne.

ABSOLUTE MONARCHY—a form of government in which the monarch holds power that is not limited by laws or a constitution.

ARISTOCRACY—an elite or upper class of society whose members hold hereditary titles or offices; a ruling class or nobility.

CONSTITUTION—a document that contains the system of fundamental laws and principles that determines the nature, functions, and limits of a government.

CONSTITUTIONAL MONARCHY—a system of government in which a monarch is guided by a constitution that specifies his or her rights, duties, and responsibilities.

CORONATION—the act or ceremony of crowning a monarch.

DEMOCRACY—a form of government in which the supreme power is retained by the people, who choose representatives through elections.

DYNASTY—a line of hereditary rulers; a succession of monarchs who are related to or members of the same family.

EMIRATE—a form of government similar to a monarchy or sultanate, in which power is in the hands of an emir, or ruler of a Muslim state.

MONARCHY—a system of government in which a monarch reigns over a state or territory, usually for life and by hereditary right.

PARLIAMENT—a legislative assembly or lawmaking body.

PARLIAMENTARY DEMOCRACY—a political system with an elected parliament, in which a prime minister serves as head of government.

PRIMOGENITURE—the law determining succession: the throne is passed down to the firstborn child.

REALM—a kingdom.

REFERENDUM—a vote by the people on a specific question.

REGENT—a person who rules when a monarch is a child or is incapacitated.

REGALIA—the emblems or symbols of royalty.

REPUBLIC—a democratic form of government in which elected representatives vote on legislation and in which the head of state isn't a monarch but is usually a president.

SOVEREIGN—a monarch.

SULTANATE—a government in which the supreme power is in the hands of a sultan (the head of a Muslim state).

FURTHER READING

FOR OLDER READERS

Carter, Miranda. *George, Nicholas and Wilhelm: Three Royal Cousins and the Road to World War One.* New York: Alfred A. Knopf, 2010.

Freeman, Philip. *Alexander the Great.* New York: Simon & Schuster, 2011.

Robinson, Francis. *The Mughal Emperors: And the Islamic Dynasties of India, Iran, Central Asia, 1206–1925.* London: Thames & Hudson, 2007.

Siler, Julia Flynn. *Lost Kingdom: Hawaii's Last Queen, the Sugar Kings, and America's First Imperial Adventure.* New York: Atlantic Monthly Press, 2012.

FOR YOUNGER READERS

Cotter, Charis. *Kids Who Rule: The Remarkable Lives of Five Child Monarchs.* Buffalo, NY: Annick Press, 2007.

Gifford, Clive. *10 Kings and Queens Who Changed the World.* New York: Kingfisher, 2009.

Kerrigan, Michael. *Mesopotamians.* New York: Benchmark, 2010.

Stefoff, Rebecca. *Monarchy.* New York: Benchmark Books, 2007.

Tyldesley, Joyce. *Chronicle of the Queens of Egypt: From Early Dynastic Times to the Death of Cleopatra.* London: Thames & Hudson, 2006.

Waldherr, Kris. *Doomed Queens: Royal Women Who Met Bad Ends, From Cleopatra to Princess Di.* New York: Three Rivers Press, 2008.

INTERNET RESOURCES

www.royal.gov.uk

The official website of the British Monarchy provides the latest news about the royal family, as well as links to the history of the monarchy, the royal collection and residences, and much more.

http://www.npr.org/2011/04/26/135413612/kings-and-queens-of-the-world-where-monarchies-still-exist

This map, from National Public Radio, shows where monarchies exist (as of 2012).

http://www.kinghussein.gov.jo/hash_intro.html

The website for the Hashemite royal family of Jordan features links to the family tree and provides background information on Islam and the royal coat of arms.

INDEX

Numbers in **bold italics** refer to captions.

CONTRIBUTORS

Senior Consulting Editor **TIMOTHY J. COLTON** is Morris and Anna Feldberg Professor of Government and Russian Studies and is the chair of the Department of Government at Harvard University. His books include *The Dilemma of Reform in the Soviet Union* (1986); *Moscow: Governing the Socialist Metropolis* (1995), which was named best scholarly book in government and political science by the Association of American Publishers; *Transitional Citizens: Voters and What Influences Them in the New Russia* (2000); and *Popular Choice and Managed Democracy: The Russian Elections of 1999 and 2000* (with Michael McFaul, 2003). Dr. Colton is a member of the editorial board of World Politics and Post-Soviet Affairs.

LEEANNE GELLETLY is the author of several books for young adults, including biographies of Harriet Beecher Stowe, Mae Jemison, Roald Dahl, Ida Tarbell, and John Marshall.